FUN WITH APPLIQUÉ

by Mira Silverstein
    Fun with Bargello
    Fun with Appliqué

FUN WITH APPLIQUÉ

by Mira Silverstein

Charles Scribner's Sons/New York

ACKNOWLEDGMENTS

I wish to thank my husband Irwin Silverstein, my sons Dean and Josh, and my daughter Elise for their help and moral support when the deadline was just around the corner and things got hectic.

Many thanks to my friend Joan Toggitt for making available to me her marvelous selection of needlework supplies.

Many thanks also to Shari and Sal Lopes for working around the clock to get the photographs ready on time and to my dear friend and assistant Ethel Tager for being there when I needed her most.

A very special thank you to Elinor Parker, my editor, for her encouragement and patience and her confidence in me.

All photographs by Salvatore Lopes
Drawings for Dragons and Scheherazade by Helen Maris
Drawings and appliqué design for Night and Day by Bonnie Belden
Drawing for "College Boards" by Dean Silverstein
Drawings for Mice by Patricia Weiss
Drawings and appliqué designs for Paisley and Parade Elephant by
    Elise Silverstein
All other designs in appliqué by Mira Silverstein
Antique silk patchwork appliqué quilt courtesy Naiomi Eisner
All other antique coverlets, fabrics, and lace courtesy Ann Holzer

Copyright © 1973 *Mira Silverstein*

This book published simultaneously in the
United States of America and in Canada—
Copyright under the Berne Convention

All rights reserved. No part of this book
may be reproduced in any form without the
permission of Charles Scribner's Sons.

1 3 5 7 9 11 13 15 17 19 D/C 20 18 16 14 12 10 8 6 4 2

Printed in the United States of America
Library of Congress Catalog Card Number 72-11144
SBN 684-13193-5 (cloth)

To Pearl Grant

Mice. These two charming little "farmers" are very good beginners' projects and ideal for using up small scraps of fabric. Appliqué bodies first. Trace and embroider faces before attaching to backing. Over-embroider pitchfork, pie, and shoes at the very end. See pages 14 and 27.

A<small>PPLIQUE STITCHING</small> may have its origin in ancient history, but to me it is most closely identified with colonial America. Economy was a way of life and it was important to save every scrap of material and render it useful. Thrifty, hardworking, inventive, warm, the women of early America were endowed with a sense of humor and a deep need for permanency. These qualities, as nothing else, are reflected in the lovely examples of old appliqué that have endured for generations.

Today, needlecraft is enjoying a renewed popularity. The sudden interest in appliqué is very exciting. The emphasis is on creative fun rather than thrift, and the finished articles are often purely decorative rather than utilitarian. New materials are plentiful and comparatively inexpensive so that it is not necessary to constantly save basketfuls of scraps. It must be very gratifying to turn some old fabric into something new and useful. But unless you love the old fabric, it's a waste of time. Appliqué, as all needlework, should be a pleasant experience—a fun project. A slight deviation in the rules, a small mistake here and there, hardly matters. What does matter is the excitement, the pleasure, and the involvement in making something you really like.

MATERIALS

Never before has there been such a wealth of materials available in the creative stitchery market.

Fabrics. New and old, first and most important. Cottons, linens, woolens, silks, and synthetics come in the most dazzling display of color and texture ever seen. For old fabrics, there is a never-ending source of supply beginning with your own storage room and that of your friends and family, to thrift and antique shops. Be on the lookout for interesting prints and textures as well as fragments of antique embroidery and beaded cloth.

Yarns and threads. The overwhelming selection of fabrics is rivaled only by that of embroidery threads found in even the most modest needlecraft shops. Here again, we have cotton, wool, silk, and synthetics as well as some lovely non-tarnishing metallics. Buy small quantities and experiment.

The most useful thread is the six-strand embroidery cotton. This is a soft, almost silky thread. Each strand subdivides into six very thin filaments that are surprisingly strong. Used singly, they are excellent for pencil-thin outlines and will not snarl as much as mercerised thread.

Beads, ribbons, and assorted trim. Beads are beautiful. One of the most exciting visual experiences is to visit a store that specializes in embroidery beads and pearls. They come in a large assortment of shapes and colors and may be purchased in small quantities.

Ribbons, lace, and trimmings are a must in your collection.

Search for and collect materials and keep an orderly file. Small see-through bags and plastic boxes are better than one large basket. As you gain experience, you will be able to identify what is useful to you and what is not. You will become selective, and at this point your stitchery will begin to reflect your own personality; this is as it should be.

TOOLS OF THE TRADE

Scissors. Very sharp and of best quality. You need two. One of medium size for cutting fabrics and one small, straight-pointed embroidery type for getting into corners and clipping threads. Find scissors that you are comfortable with and then call them your own.

Needles. The selection is very large. Buy several kinds and more than one in each variety. There are lovely thin embroidery needles, milliner needles, and crewel needles with larger eyes and heavier shafts that accommodate the thicker yarns. If you want to work with beads, don't overlook the hair-thin beading needles. Do not use tapestry needles for appliqué because they have blunt points and will damage your fabrics.

Pins. Absolutely indispensable. Keep a large supply on hand.

Large pin cushion

A small magnet. Helpful in tracking down scattered pins.

Tracing paper. Large sheets of very sheer tracing paper in pads or rolls are available in art supply stores. Dressmaker transfer paper in blue and white and chalk pencils are available in dressmaker supply stores.

Fine marking pens

Cellophane tape

Paper paste or glue

Ruler

Iron

A smooth hard board the size of your appliqué or larger

Tacks or sharp pushpins

METHOD

Appliqué stitchery, in essence, is the art of cutting out fabric or fabrics in different shapes and sewing them to another fabric which serves as a background. Sometimes these cut-outs are over-embroidered with stitchery. This helps to identify and elaborate the pattern.

The basic steps are simple. Size of appliqué is predetermined. Design is chosen and enlarged or reduced to required size. Fabrics are selected. Design is then copied on a sheet of tracing paper and transferred to the background fabric. Design is also transferred in parts on the various pieces of fabric to be used as appliqué. The pieces of fabric are cut out and carefully pinned to their outline on the background. Afterward, they are basted, stitched firmly, and over-embroidered.

Now, let's take these steps one at a time.

Establish the size of the finished appliqué and allow at least three inches all around for margin.

Design. There are two basic ways to create a design for appliqué. One is to use a given drawing, the other is to assemble a design of cutout shapes or parts from various designs. Move these pieces around on a paper background until they form a composition that you like. Tack them in place with a dab of glue and you have an original design. Keep designs simple at first. Bear in mind that each piece will have to be cut out, pinned, basted, and stitched, and so the simpler the outline, the better. You can always use over-embroidery to elaborate a design.

Once your design is established, place a sheet of sheer tracing paper over it, pin it in place, and, using a fine-line marker, trace the entire design. At this point you can simplify lines and omit areas that are of no interest to you. The design may be enlarged with a photostat. This is a very accurate means of reproducing a design and is comparatively inexpensive. A design can also be enlarged by dividing it in small squares of equal size and copying it one square at a time on the larger surface which has been divided into the same number of squares.

If your design is enlarged from the tracing paper, you must then trace it again. There are many advantages in working with patterns that have been drawn on tracing paper. Patterns may be reversed, and small portions of your design can be copied by simply placing another sheet of tracing paper over your pattern and retracing it. This may be done while the original pattern is still pinned to the fabric. In addition, tracing paper is lightweight, easy to store, and inexpensive—so that at the slightest sign of wear, simply retrace on a fresh sheet of paper. (Small sheets of tracing paper may be joined with cellophane tape.)

Outline the final pattern with four straight sides. This frames out the picture. It gives you a definite dimension and it helps in lining up the design whenever you must retrace.

Select fabrics with care. If your appliqué is to be washed, color-fast, permanent-press fabrics are highly recommended. For decorative appliqué you may choose from a larger selection of available fabrics. If they are smooth and soft and don't ravel easily, allow one-fourth-inch margin for folding under appliqué. If fabric is coarse and tends to ravel and you simply must use it for that special effect, cut out the pattern without leaving the one-fourth-inch allowance, fasten to backing with small running stitches, and cover rough outline with a heavy embroidery such as a satin or buttonhole stitch or use a cord or other trim.

Background fabric should be large enough to accommodate the entire design. If the backround must be pieced, it is best to incorporate the seams into the appliqué pattern. The fabric used for the background must be heavier than the one used for the appliqué. Sometimes, as in the case of a large wallhanging, an extra piece of fabric is used under the background for additional support. This may be some heavy muslin or linen or even some old drapery fabric. Press all fabrics before using.

Stretch the background fabric over a flat smooth board that will take tacks or pushpins without splitting. Pin it down around the edges with sharp pushpins. Place the transfer paper shiny side down on fabric. (If the sheets are small, place several side by side to cover the entire design area. Don't tape them.) Now place the tracing paper with the design on it on top of the transfer paper and pin it to prevent it from shifting.

Trace the entire design using a soft pencil or pointed wooden stick. It is not necessary to trace the parts that will be over-embroidered at this point, unless they extend into the background.

Remove the papers and design outlines. If necessary, correct and sharpen detail with a chalk pencil. Both transfer papers and chalk pencils are available in dark and light colors. Using the above method, transfer all the parts of

See pages 6 and 27.

the design that will be used in appliqué on the various pieces of fabric selected. This time transfer over-embroidery outlines as well.

Remove papers and cut out each piece of fabric to be appliquéd with a small, pointed, sharp scissors. Cut carefully, following design outline, and allow one-fourth-inch margin for folding under. If any fabrics do not take transfer lines, copy the outline on a separate piece of tracing paper, pin it to the fabric, and cut out *both* paper and fabric at one time. Remember to leave the extra margin. If you are working with many small fabric pieces, you will find it helpful to leave the paper tracings pinned to the individual fabric cutouts until ready to use.

Remove paper patterns from all appliqué fabric pieces and pin each to its own outline. This is the time to reevaluate the choice of colors and textures. Sometimes it is a good idea to let a design "rest" for a day or two before making the final decision. The best part of appliqué stitchery is the complete freedom it affords. You can move pieces of fabric around, eliminate some, change colors, and come up with something that is truly yours, an original creation.

Basting. Once you decide to go ahead with the design, remove the appliqué design from the board and start basting the fabric pieces to the background. Basting is a very important step in appliqué stitchery. If it is done properly, the pins can be removed and the whole fabric handled with ease for as long as necessary. Fold under the one-fourth-inch excess fabric as you baste. Use the point of the needle as a tool. Whenever the fabric curves, clip a few times along the curve, almost to the fold line. Do the same in the corners (see diagram page 16). Baste with small running stitches, very close to the edge of the appliqué, and if possible use thread of a distinctive color so that it can be identi-

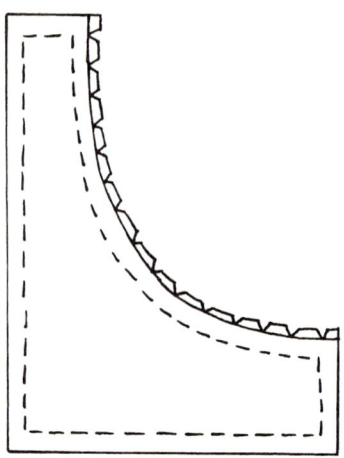

If a piece of appliqué curves, notch fabric along the curve (up to but not through fold line). Fold fabric under using the needle as a tool, and pin, baste, and stitch in place.

fied easily when you cut. Knot the basting thread and leave the knot on the right side of the fabric. As you finish a length of thread, fasten it with one or two tacks, also on the right side. Before removing the basting threads, cut away the knots and pull out tacks with the point of the needle, then clip the thread every inch or so and pull out the pieces very gently. If the thread resists, often because some embroidery stitches "stepped" over it, cut it away carefully. Never pull or tug at basting thread because it will pucker the fabric and could ruin a lovely appliqué. When you finish basting, remove all the pins. Fasten all the basted pieces with blind stitches or tiny running stitches. Use single-strand embroidery thread, matching it as closely to the fabric as possible.

It is important to practice all the stitches described on pages 52-56. The tiny blind stitches will give you a virtually

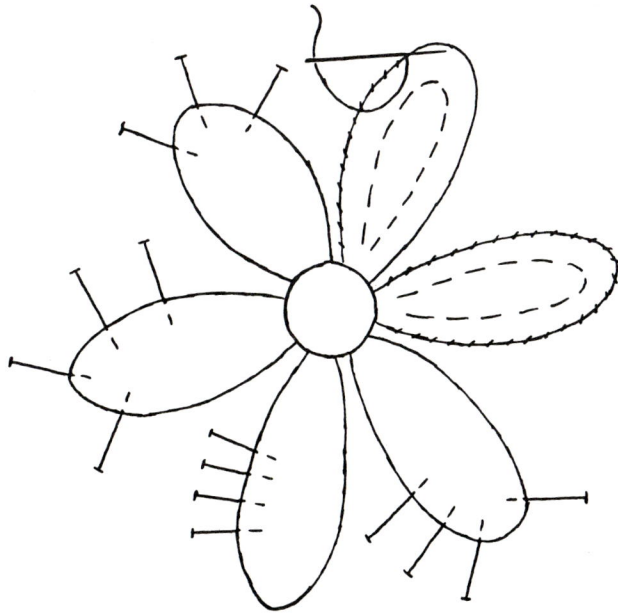

Blind stitching is a most effective way to fasten appliqué fabric. It is a tiny stitch, almost invisible when using threads in matching colors. Use fine thread and needle. Take a tiny stitch through both fabrics very close to the edge of the appliqué and pull firmly. Blind stitching tends to puff out appliqué and is very effective in flower or figure designs.

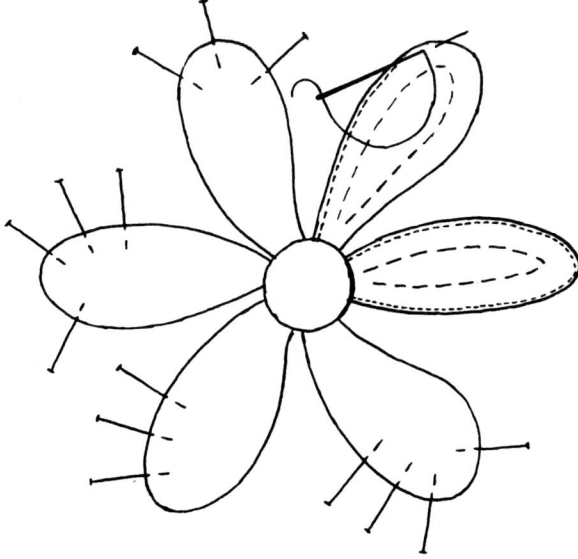

invisible outline and will cause the appliqué to puff out, giving it a slightly raised look. This is especially nice when working on flowers or small figures. A running stitch will be more visible and will fasten the appliqué flat against the background. A little practice will help you keep the stitches even. For a bolder outline use buttonhole or satin stitch.

If the appliqué is in layers, that is, if several pieces of fabric overlap with only a part of each showing through, baste the first layer and appliqué only the part of the design that will show. The part that will remain hidden may be left with the basting thread on. Then it should be cut away. Each subsequent layer of fabric is applied the same way. The Scheherazade on pages 32 and 35 is a good example of layered appliqué. The Paisley (pages 28 and 38) is also appliquéd in layers, but in a slightly different manner. Here the same design outline is appliquéd over another one

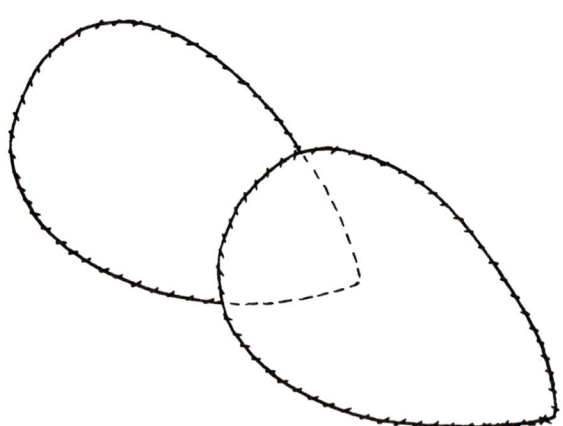

If one piece of appliqué overlaps another, it is not necessary to fold under the part that is covered by the overlapping piece.

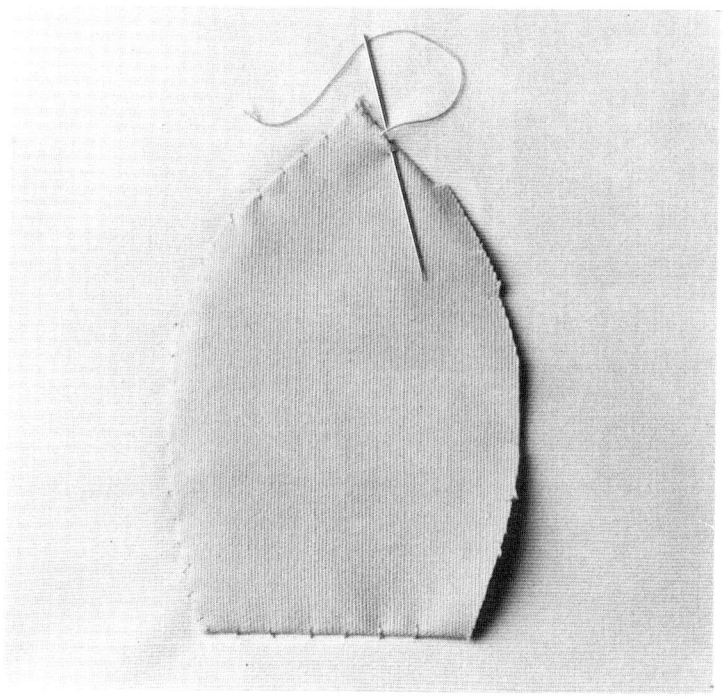

that is slightly larger. Each layer is completely visible and is stitched all around. This produces a cushioned look, and when worked with velvet it is elegant. When the appliqué is finished, check and clip loose threads and remove basting stitches wherever they are visible.

Over-embroider as you see fit. This is where the creative part comes in. Don't overdo the stitchery. Remember that embroidery is meant to enhance the appliqué and not overwhelm it.

Do have fun with appliqué stitchery. Try your hand at creating your own designs. Experiment with different types of fabric. You will find that some silky fabrics are slippery and may require an extra line of basting to hold them in place. Velvets are not suitable for very small designs because the nap in the fabric tends to overshadow a small outline. They look magnificent on larger areas, and if you ever wondered what to do with some of the lovely velvet in an old evening gown, look again at the Paisley (pages 28 and 38) or the Parade Elephant (page 37).

Teach the youngsters to work with appliqué. Let them start with felt. This is non-woven fabric that does not ravel and does not require folding under. Children love to cut out simple shapes and sew them with large stitches in bold colors.

Banners are excellent projects for appliqué. Try, also, copying a coat of arms using antique brocade and gold braid. A number of heraldic books are available in libraries and book stores that offer information on the design and history of banners and coats of arms.

Make something that looks familiar. Save bits of fabric from some of your favorite things and work them into your appliqué designs. Family portraits are fun to do. Use simple outlines for depicting figures. Newspaper fashion pages are the best sources of design ideas for this. Identify figures with bits of fabric from familiar clothing, color and outline of hair, pipes, toys, or pets. Using the same principle you can design wallhangings that tell a familiar story or show highlights from a vacation. Involve the whole family in such a project.

Make a wallhanging with pockets in different shapes and sizes. Appliqué each pocket with a picture that indicates what belongs inside (doll, car, book, block, etc.). Make pockets roomy and very colorful.

Illustrations from children's books, enlarged and traced or copied freehand, are excellent appliqué ideas for children's rooms. A favorite story or story character made into a wallhanging or pillow is great.

PATCHWORK

I would like to say a few words about patchwork, since it is closely related to appliqué. The small pieces of fabric are sewn to each other to form a large unit. Sometimes a number of squares of fabric are worked in appliqué and then joined together to form a large piece of fabric. This is used as is or lined for extra strength.

Patchwork is used largely for quilts and coverlets, although today many accessories and articles of clothing are made in patchwork fabric.

On pages 24 and 25 are four examples of antique patchwork.

Do a friendship patchwork. Everyone does an original appliqué on a square of fabric. Join all the squares to form a large wallhanging or line it and make a coverlet. For added interest, a large patchwork design may be assembled from segments that are not similar in size and shape.

If you wish to try your hand at quiltmaking, there are a number of excellent books available on this subject.

No other form of art needlework leaves so much room for creative expression as appliqué stitchery. The rules are few and flexible. Materials are inexpensive and fun to acquire. As you work in appliqué you make your own rules and your own discoveries. It is a beautiful experience.

Have fun with appliqué!

Patchwork coverlet. Make triangles by cutting a square into four equal parts. These triangles form the base of some very interesting geometric patterns. They may be joined with machine stitching to form a large piece of fabric or worked in appliqué with small running stitches on a backing of muslin.

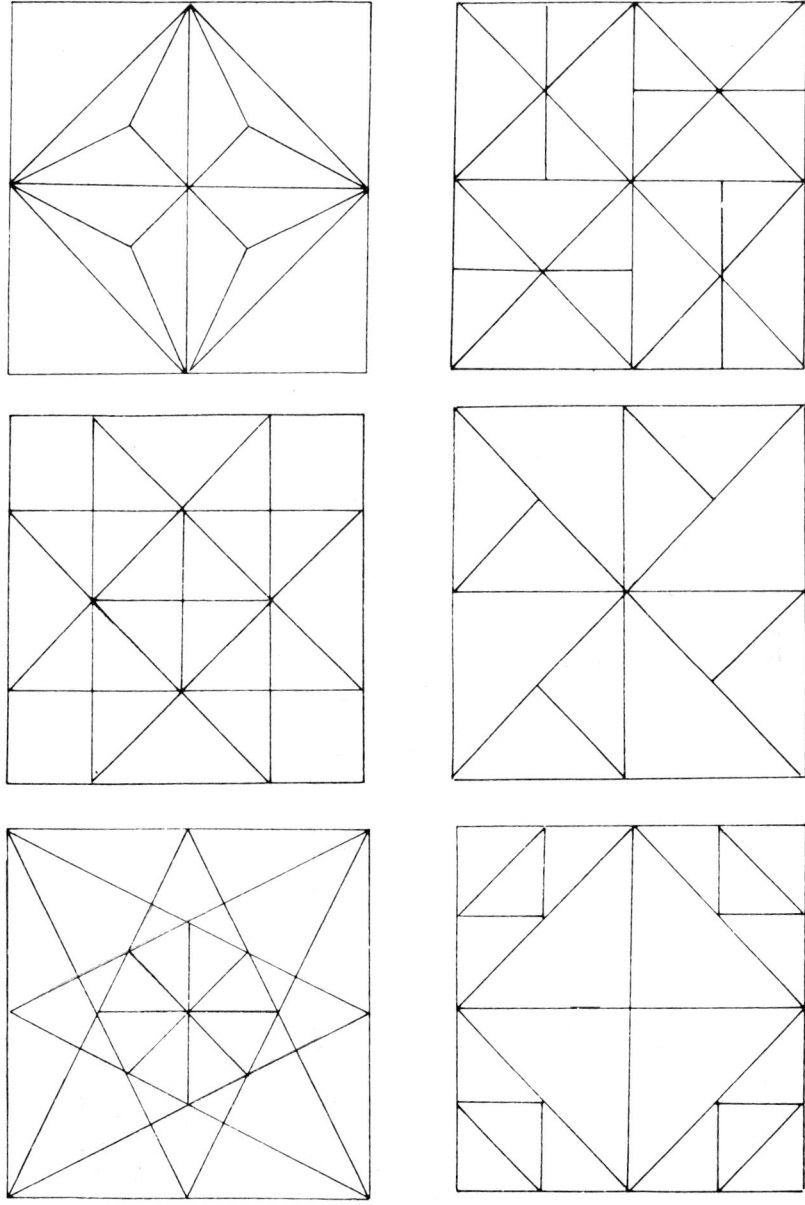

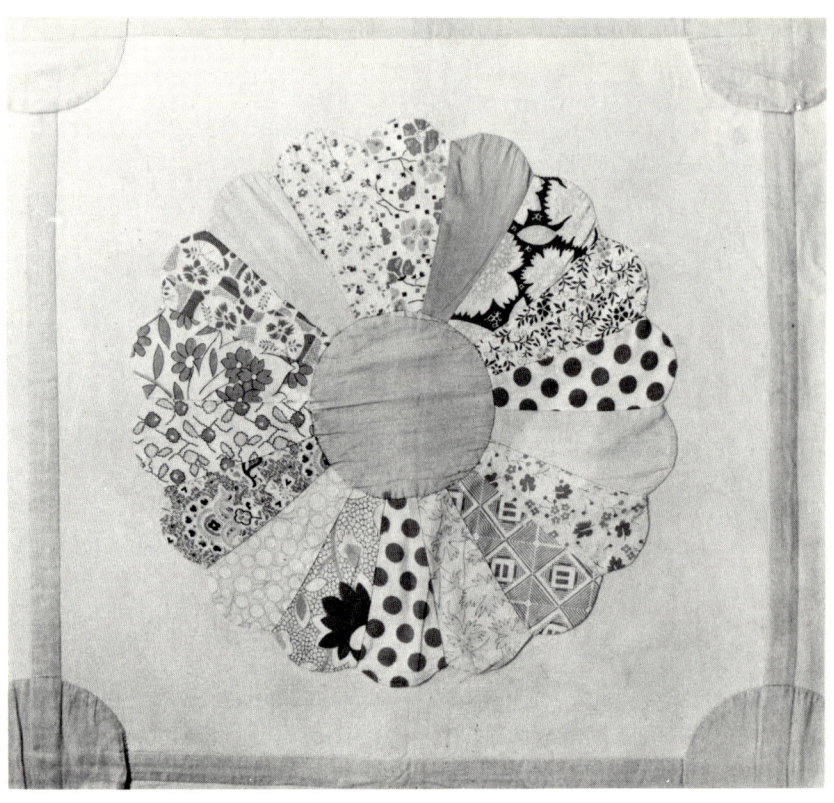

Detail from antique bedspread. Each flower is worked in appliqué on a square of muslin. Muslin squares are then joined to form a bedspread or coverlet. Lining is optional.

Antique crazy quilt made from small pieces of fine fabrics. Bits of lace, silk, scraps from antique fabrics and ribbons are blind stitched in an irregular pattern on 6" x 6" squares of muslin. Allow one-fourth-inch seam allowance on muslin squares, but don't let the muslin show between the pieces of appliqué. Join all the squares to form a large piece of fabric. This one was lined with red velveteen. A fabric such as this may be used to make a magnificent skirt or vest or even a handbag. Cut the pattern from muslin or similar fabric. Indicate the darts and seam allowance with basting stitches. Appliqué the entire fabric area with small pieces of fine fabric. Remove basting stitches. Press flat and finish according to pattern instructions.

See pages 6 and 14.

See page 37.

See page 38.

See pages 42-43.

Night and Day. Sky was appliquéd and over-embroidered on background fabric. Hills and valleys were worked in appliqué separately, on a heavy piece of muslin. The pieces of fabric were layered to create a sculptured effect. They were then placed against the sky and fastened with blind stitches. The finished appliqué was stretched on a small board cut in the shape of a half circle. See pages 40-41.

Scheherazade. A fairy tale translated in appliqué. This seemingly ambitious project is really quite simple to do. I used a heavy backing of some leftover upholstery fabric 30" x 40". Since I meant to cover the entire surface of this fabric with appliqué, it did not matter what color I used. The backing was pinned and stretched on a large board. A light blue sateen was placed over the backing to simulate the sky. It was pressed flat and pinned to the board. The outline of the entire design was transferred on the blue fabric with white transfer paper. I traced over all the trees and grass outlines with a dark chalk pencil (you may use a fine-line felt pen), then I placed two layers of green organdy over the blue sky, making sure all the trees and grass were covered.

The throne was cut out from two different gold fabrics and placed on its outline. A dark blue silk was placed in the center and the outline of the king traced on it in white transfer paper. As the layers of different fabric cutouts were placed on the backing, they were pinned in place with straight pins. The dancing platform was cut from a piece of printed silk and the border was made from ribbons and trim. After all the pieces of fabric were pinned in place, the entire appliqué was removed from the board and the fabrics were basted and appliquéd. If the fabric could be folded under, I used blind stitches. If it could not be folded, I outlined it with gold braid which was carefully sewn to cover the raw edges. The trees and grass were outlined in a very simple manner. A small running stitch was worked over the lines visible through the two thicknesses of green organdy. I used a single strand of embroidery cotton. A second outline of embroidery, this time using the full six strands, was worked in chain stitch. After tree and grass were outlined, I cut away the organdy very close to the chain stitch outline. The effect was exactly what I wanted. The tree was very effective, yet simple, and it did not compete with the other patterns in the appliqué.

The entire wallhanging was replaced and pinned on the original board and, lining up the pattern, I retraced all the figures. This time only the outlines were needed. Each figure was then traced in detail on pieces of muslin. Each piece was large enough to accommodate a complete figure. The faces were embroidered in back stitch and the hair in little straight stitches, using single-strand thread. The clothing was cut out from scraps of fine fabrics and pinned, basted, and stitched to the figures. Each figure, fully dressed, was pinned individually to its outline. Appliqué was removed from the board and blind stitched. Very special care was taken to stitch the faces and hands. In order to achieve the "fullness" in the turban and tunic worn by the king I cut a larger piece of fabric than needed. It was stitched on three sides and the excess fabric was "draped" and folded under on the fourth side.

Beading and over-embroidery were done last. All stitching and over-embroidery were done through all the thicknesses of the fabrics. As you can see, the overall design was simplified and some parts were either changed or omitted. The entire design may be simplified. For example, the dancing girl may dance under the tree with only one or two musicians in attendance. The throne may be omitted and the tree made larger and fuller. Detail of one figure below.

Turtle. This is one of the easiest appliqués in this book and may be used as a first project. An 18" x 18" square of green velveteen was backed with a square of leftover fabric of the same size. Both fabrics were pinned together and the turtle (enlarged to 14" x 14") was traced on the green. The head, body, and feet were outlined with a straight machine stitch which formed a "pocket" between the two fabrics. This pocket was padded slightly to bring the turtle outline in relief, as follows: two or three small slits were made on the underside and small bits of cotton wool were inserted with a long narrow stick. Padding may be as heavy or as light as you wish. The rest of the turtle was cut out from a piece of printed fabric, pinned, basted, and stitched to its outline. Over-embroidery was done in chain stitch and French knots. See page 26.

Parade Elephant. A very simple, fun-to-do appliqué. Two 18" x 18" squares of velvet were used. Since it is sometimes difficult to trace on velvet, the elephant pattern was pinned to the turquoise velvet and cut out. The velvet elephant was then pinned to the wine-colored backing. As the design is all in one piece, it was not necessary to trace the outline again on the background. There is one-fourth-inch margin for folding under. The pattern was pinned and basted, then stitched with blind stitches in matching threads. It was heavily over-embroidered with a four-ply rayon thread in chain stitch, sequins, and pearls. The elephant's ear was cut out separately (two pieces, see pattern), machine-stitched on the wrong side, turned right side out, and fastened to the top of the head with concealed stitches. The ear may also be cut out as a piece of appliqué and stitched to the head of the elephant. See page 29.

Paisley. This simple pattern has one outline. This was enlarged in several sizes and appliquéd in velvet. The center was embroidered with beads, pearls, sequins, and simple embroidery stitches, mostly chain and long straight. The outlines were done in a very even, widely spaced, blanket stitch. This appliqué was made entirely by hand. See page 28.

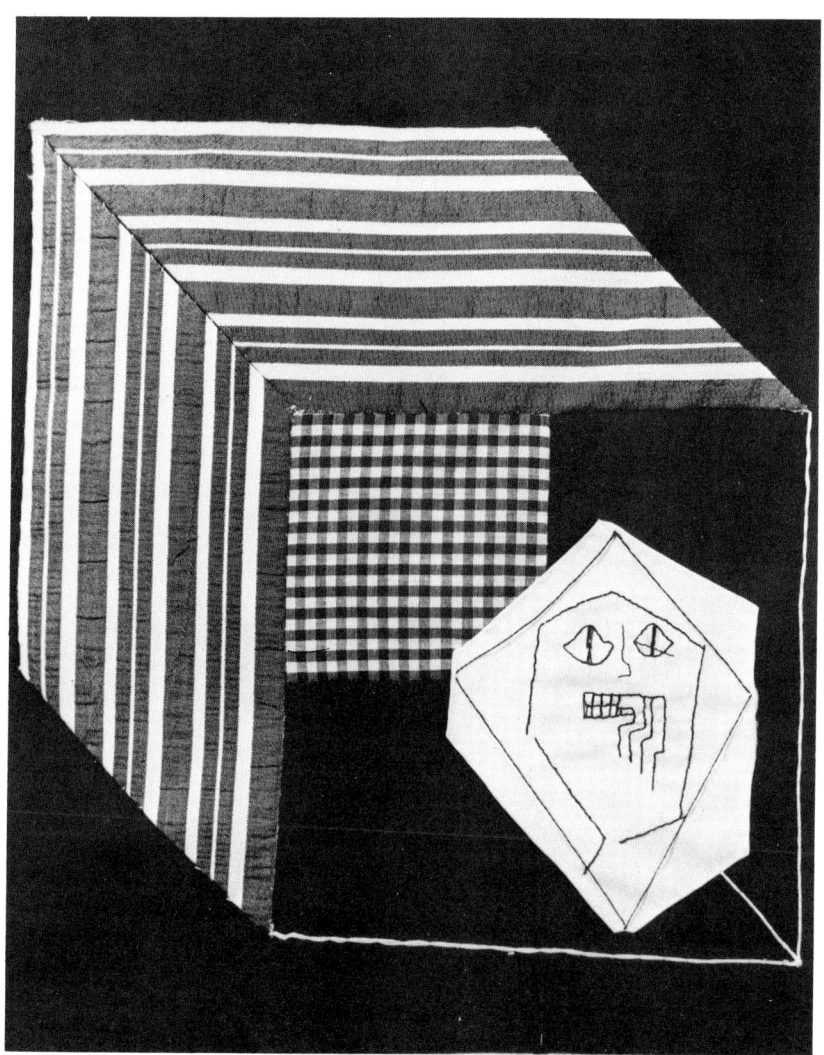

College Boards. This is a doodle lifted from my son's doodling pad. It was copied exactly and outlined in black outline stitch using one strand of the six-strand cotton embroidery thread. The face was outlined with four large stitches. The "cube" was cut and assembled from pieces of black and white cotton fabric. The two white lines are couched white six-strand embroidery cotton.

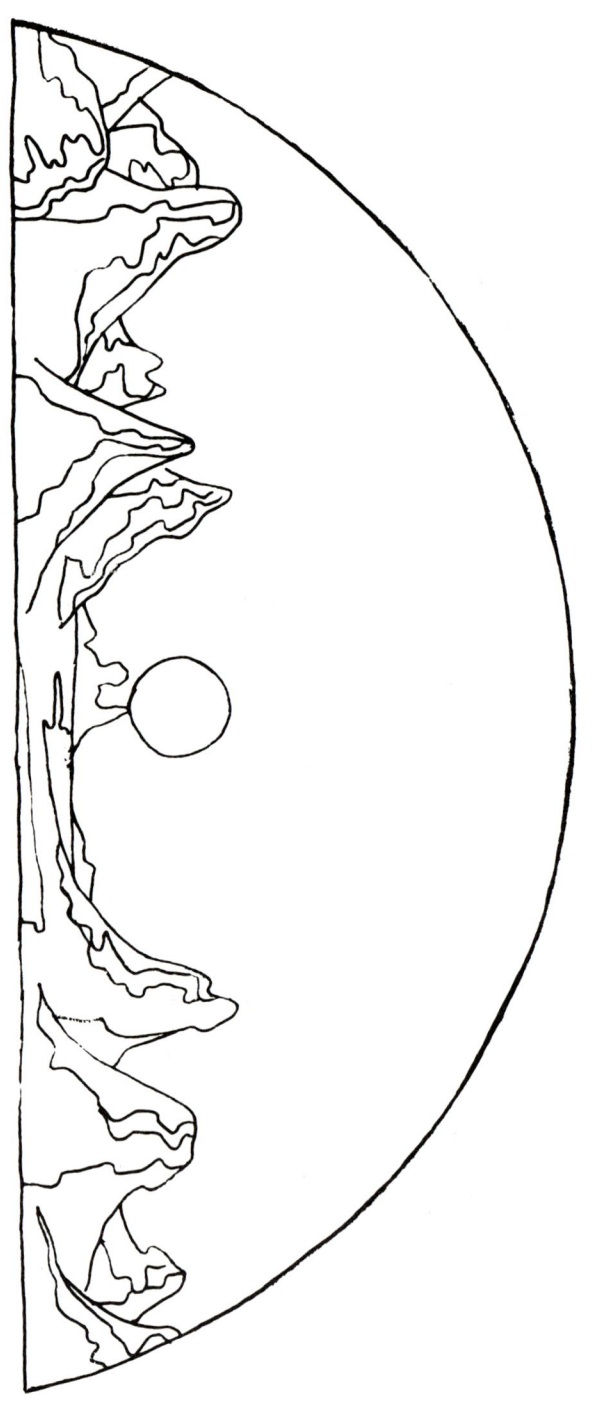

40

See page 31.

Dragons. This is a large wallhanging measuring 65″ x 30″. It used two yards of blue crepe and three-fourths of a yard each of pale green and pale pink sateen. The blue crepe was backed with muslin for extra weight and the dragons outlined on it. Each dragon was then traced and cut out in one piece, pinned and basted to the back-

ground, and outlined with a firm buttonhole stitch. Over-embroidery was made with simple chain stitch, outline, and open blanket stitch. Beads, sequins, and pearls were added for extra color and dimension.

This appliqué may be made smaller and in different fabrics. Also, each dragon can be used as an individual design. See page 30.

Butterfly. The white butterfly was appliquéd on a black and white printed fabric; the black one, on a solid yellow background and over-embroidered in black. This is a very simple design and I recommend it as a first project.

Black and White. This design was worked in cutout appliqué. The design was traced on the white fabric. Four additional layers of fabric of equal weight were added and basted together with the white. The medium gingham was used as the background and the white was left topside. Basting was done with large running stitches across the width of the fabric at one-inch intervals. The outline of the design was then carefully machine-stitched in one row of open zigzag followed by two rows of closed zigzag. The layers of fabric were then cut away with sharp, pointed scissors, revealing the various layers of fabric according to pattern. Another row of close zigzag was added for a smooth even outline. Loose threads were trimmed and basting carefully removed. Eyes were embroidered with black satin stitches.

This design can be enlarged to poster size and the colors varied.

Appliqué Frog. An amusing pillow to make in any size or fabric. These were made in felt, green for the body and yellow for the mouth lining and flowers.

Enlarge pattern pieces to desired size. Cut two separate pieces marked B. (This is the back.) Place pattern marked F on fold of fabric and cut one piece. (This is the underside.) Cut two pieces marked M in contrasting color. (This is the mouth lining.) Cut two circles in white fabric and two smaller ones in black for the eyes. Cut out flowers for appliqué.

Stitch both patterns marked B on the dotted line. Appliqué flowers in random design. Over-embroider, or use your own decorative appliqué or beads. Assemble eyes by placing small black circles inside white ones and attach to head where indicated. Use blind stitches and matching thread.

Place each half of mouth lining marked M to its own half of body pattern, right sides in. Stitch on dotted lines and turn each right side out. Do not press. Line up the head parts and pin the mouth closed. Now fold back the body pattern to reveal the two straight sides of the mouth lining and stitch them together. Remove pins. Line up B and F and pin together. Leave mouth open. Since the back of frog is slightly curved, it will have to be "eased" into place. This pattern is a very simple one, so that there is no need for notches. Baste, remove pins, and machine stitch leaving a side opening for stuffing. Stuff with your favorite batting, as firm or as soft as you like. Slip stitch side opening. Adjust mouth with a few invisible tacks at each end.

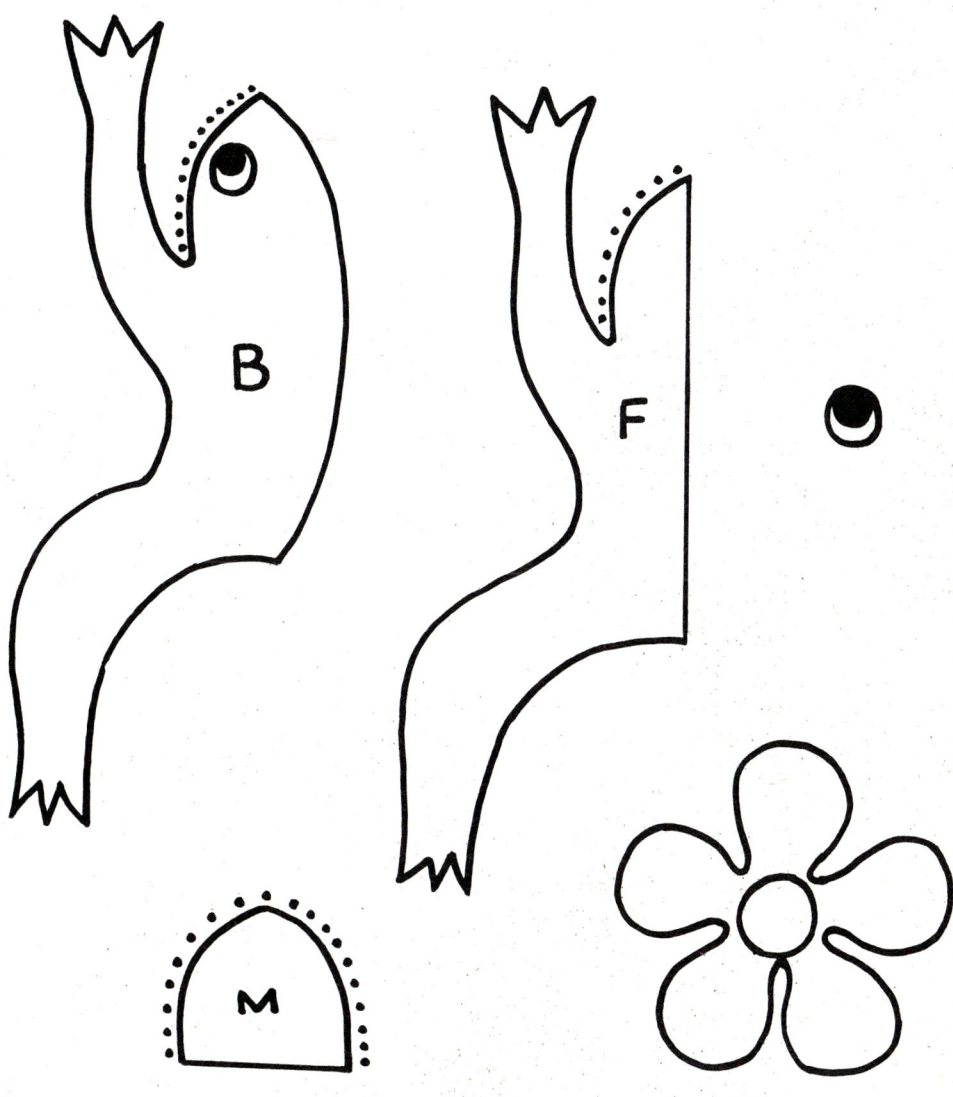

Puppets with appliqué faces are great fun and very easy to do. Enlarge basic puppet outline to measure 17″ from top to bottom and 8½″ from left to right. Use felt for best results. Cut two pieces for each puppet, appliqué face with felt cutouts, and stitch the two pieces by hand or machine, leaving the bottom hem open. Yarn hair or a tiny hat complete your puppet. If you want to dress the puppet, make a simple jumper (see pattern) in bright colors or prints and slip it over the puppet's head.

Puppets for children should be as simple as possible and leave lots of room for imagination. It is a good idea to have several cutouts in different shapes for the eyes, mouth, and nose of puppet. Place two small circles of black felt on top of two larger circles of white felt to make the eyes. Move the black circles about until you achieve the proper "expression." Add the eyebrows, nose, and mouth (smiling or pouting). Let the children help. Once the face looks right, fasten the pieces with the proper appliqué stitches. Buttons and over-embroidery may also be used to outline the face of a puppet. Remember to use strong threads and firm stitches on all puppets.

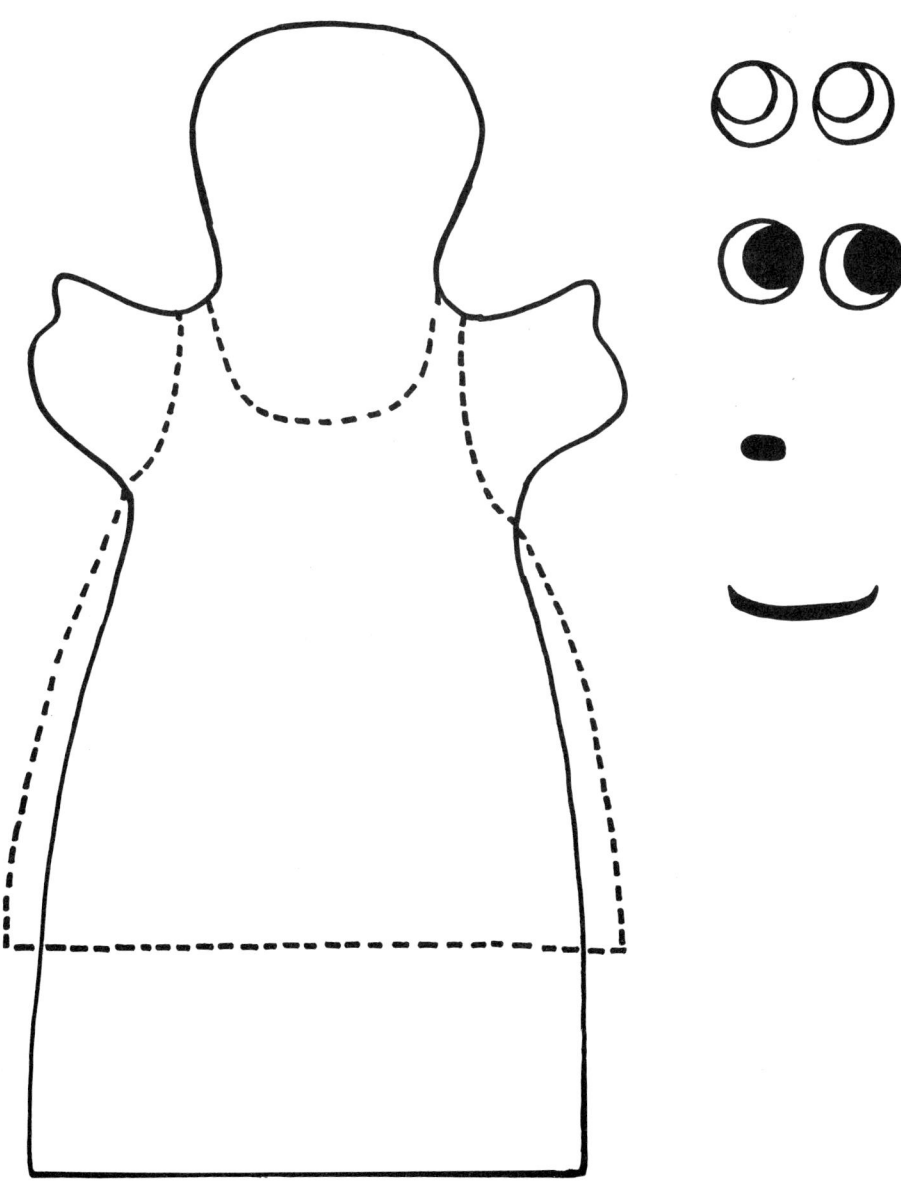

Running stitch is the simplest of stitches. The needle goes in and out of the fabric at fairly equal intervals. This is used as the basting stitch. When tacking down appliqué, make stitches fairly small. Some very lovely designs are achieved in appliqué stitchery with running stitches in various colors.

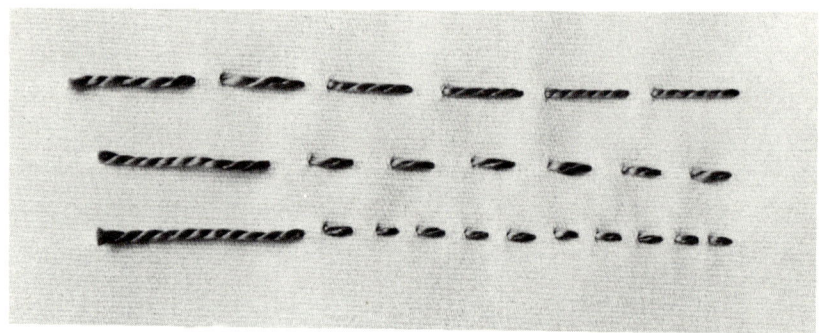

Chain stitch is a very decorative and useful stitch in appliqué over-embroidery. It "snakes" easily and may be used as a fill-in for special effects. Practice this stitch in order to master a graceful line with even rounded loops.

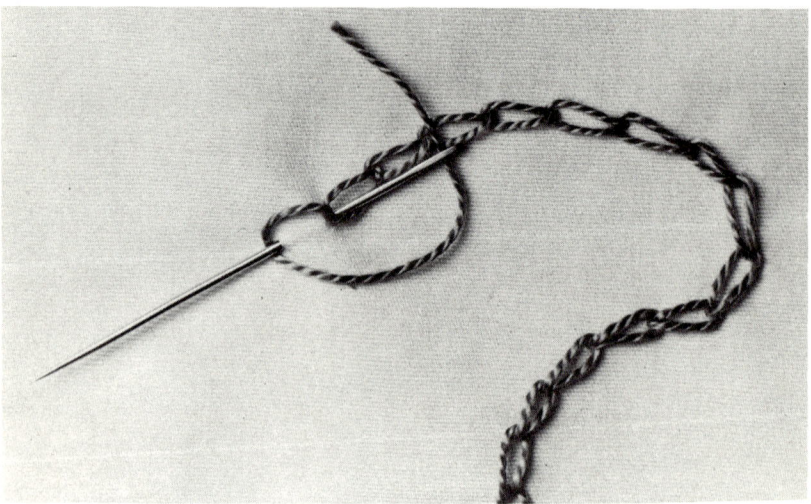

Buttonhole stitch is worked with the needle held vertically. Like all chain stitches the thread is looped under the needle point. You work it from left to right around the edge of the appliqué. It is especially good on heavy fabrics that tend to ravel. When the stitches are worked a little wider apart, you are doing blanket stitch. This can be attractive in very heavy yarn.

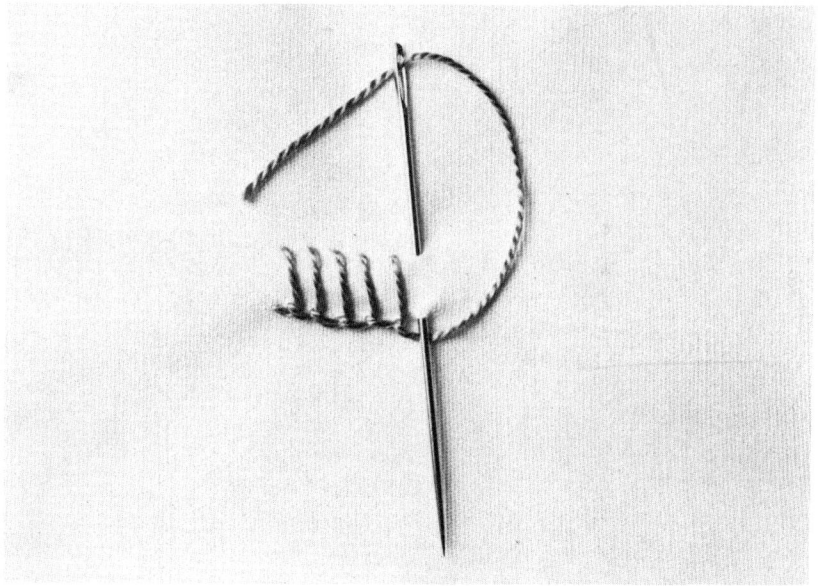

Herringbone stitch is worked from left to right as the outline indicates. It looks best when the stitches are evenly spaced, and is very good for joining patches.

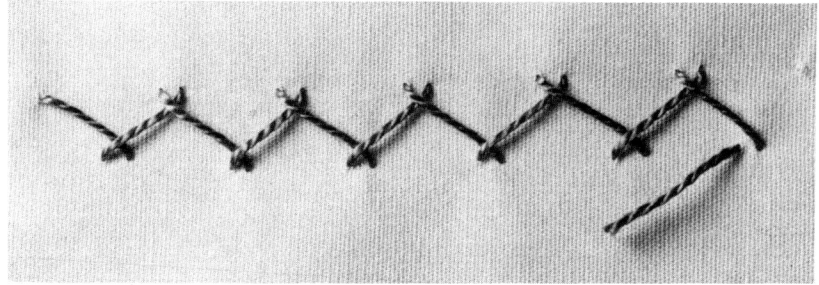

Feather stitch is a variation of the buttonhole. The needle is inserted on a slant and each stitch is a little lower than the previous one. When you slant your needle from right to left, the loops move to the right. Reverse loops by slanting needle from left to right. Loops in feather stitching should be slightly uneven.

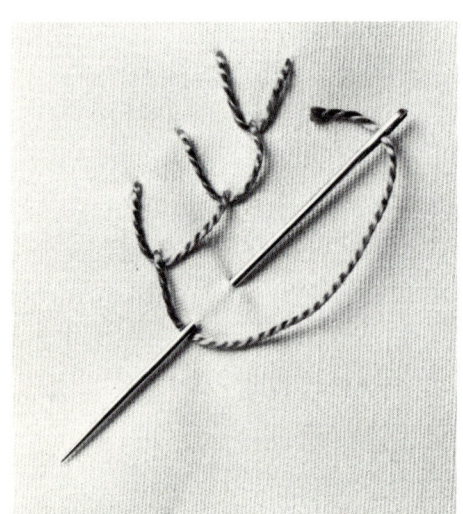

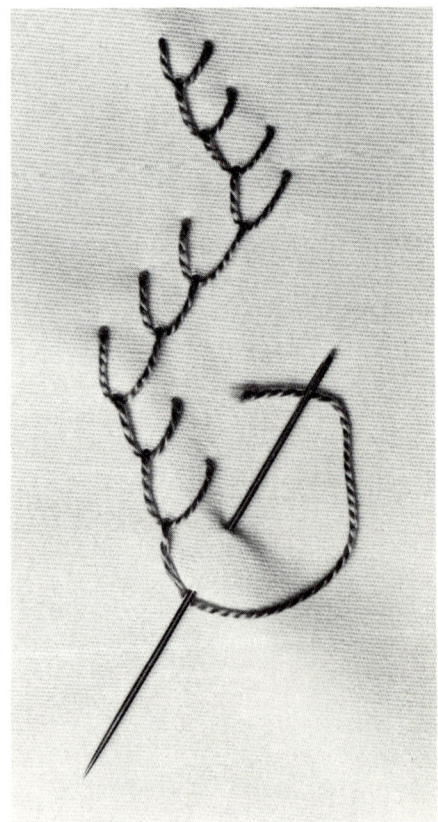

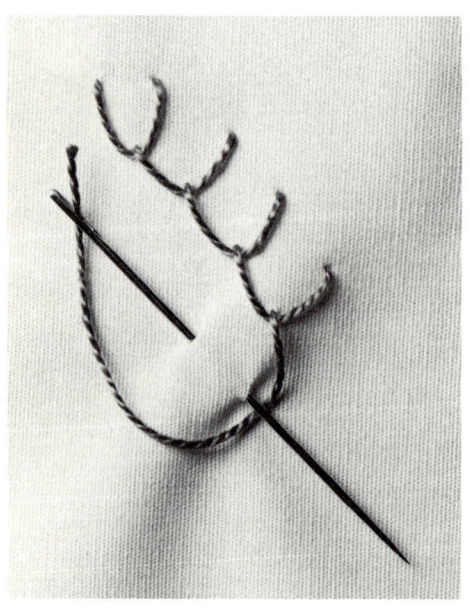

Stem stitch is also worked from left to right. If you look closely, you will see that it is a flattened version of the herringbone. Again, the stitches should be fairly even. I suggest you practice first.

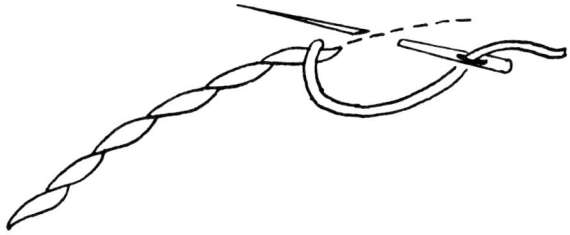

Straight stitch may be worked from right to left or left to right. If the stitches are close together, it is called satin stitch. For best results the stitches should be very even. Very nice for outlines.

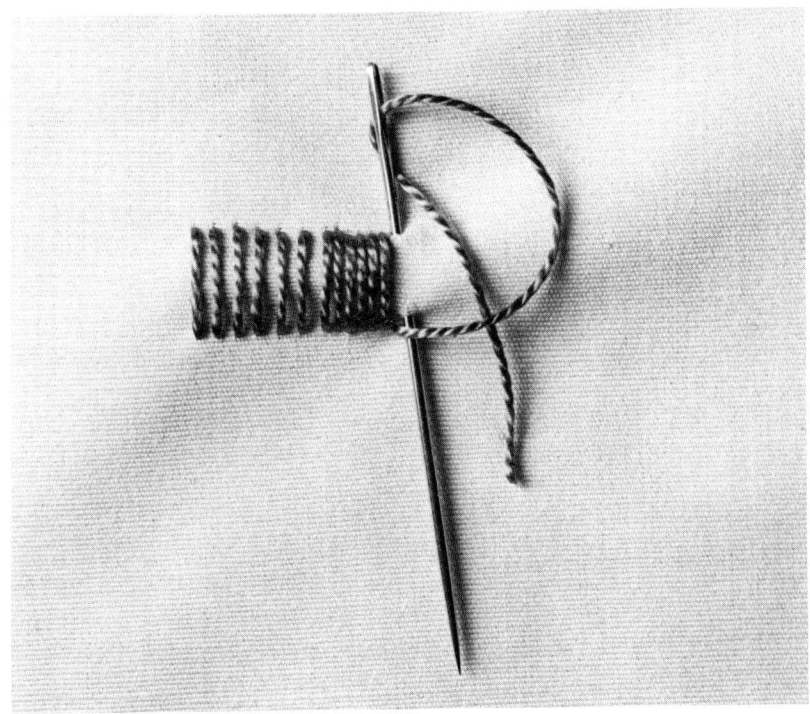

Back stitch is worked from right to left. Practice making very even stitches. Use an under and over motion and make sure that the needle is reinserted in the exact spot where it first came through. This is an excellent stitch for pencil-thin outlines.

Couching. Lay a strand of yarn on the line of the design and with another thread tie it down at equal intervals with a tiny stitch into the fabric. Try working with two threads of different colors or textures.

Beading on appliqué is a very simple procedure. It is almost like a back stitch in reverse. Insert needle into fabric, thread bead on the needle, reinsert needle into the fabric very close to the point of exit, but be sure to allow space for the bead. This is very important when using long beads. Bring needle under the fabric to the right of the bead and repeat. Make sure your needle is thin enough to accommodate the beads. Work sequins the same way. If you intend to use a lot of beads, it is a good idea to sew them through all the thicknesses of fabric you are using. Beads can be heavy and will tend to pull your appliqué design out of shape unless properly fastened.

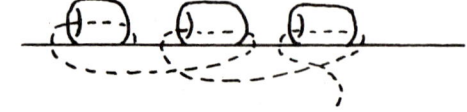